# Adult MAD LIBS®

### The world's greatest *drinking* game

# Ode to Alcohol Mad Libs

by Sarah Fabiny

Mad Libs
An Imprint of Penguin Random House

5 7 9 10 8 6
ISBN 9780843182378

Penguin supports copyright. Copyright fuels creativity, encourages diverse voices, promotes free speech, and creates a vibrant culture. Thank you for buying an authorized edition of this book and for complying with copyright laws by not reproducing, scanning, or distributing any part of it in any form without permission. You are supporting writers and allowing Penguin to continue to publish books for every reader.

Printed in the USA.

345 Hudson Street, New York, New York 10014,
an imprint of Penguin Random House LLC,
This edition published in 2014 by Mad Libs.
First published in 2013 as part of the *Party Your (Blank) Off! Box Set*.

Concept created by Roger Price & Leonard Stern

MAD LIBS
An Imprint of Penguin Random House LLC

# INSTRUCTIONS

The world's greatest *drinking* game

MAD LIBS® is a game for people who don't like games!
It can be played by one, two, three, four, or forty.

## • RIDICULOUSLY SIMPLE DIRECTIONS

In this book, you'll find stories containing blank spaces where words are left out. One player, the READER, selects one of the stories. The READER shouldn't tell anyone what the story is about. Instead, the READER should ask the other players, the WRITERS, to give words to fill in the blank spaces in the story.

## • TO PLAY

The READER asks each WRITER in turn to call out words—adjectives or nouns or whatever the spaces call for—and uses them to fill in the blank spaces in the story. The result is your very own MAD LIBS! Then, when the READER reads the completed MAD LIBS to the other players, they will discover they have written a story that is fantastic, screamingly funny, shocking, silly, crazy, or just plain dumb—depending on the words each WRITER called out.

## • EXAMPLE (*Before* and *After*)

" _____ !" he said _____
           EXCLAMATION                                    ADVERB

as he jumped into his convertible _____ and
                                                    NOUN

drove off with his _____ wife.
                              ADJECTIVE

" *Ouch* !" he said *stupidly*
           EXCLAMATION                                    ADVERB

as he jumped into his convertible *cat* and
                                                    NOUN

drove off with his *brave* wife.
                              ADJECTIVE

In case you have forgotten what adjectives, adverbs, nouns, and verbs are, here is a quick review:

An **ADJECTIVE** describes something or somebody. *Lumpy*, *soft*, *ugly*, *messy*, and *short* are adjectives.

An **ADVERB** tells how something is done. It modifies a verb and usually ends in "ly." *Modestly*, *stupidly*, *greedily*, and *carefully* are adverbs.

A **NOUN** is the name of a person, place, or thing. *Sidewalk*, *umbrella*, *bridle*, *bathtub*, and *nose* are nouns.

A **VERB** is an action word. *Run*, *pitch*, *jump*, and *swim* are verbs. Put the verbs in past tense if the directions say **PAST TENSE**. *Ran*, *pitched*, *jumped*, and *swam* are verbs in the past tense.

When we ask for **A PLACE**, we mean any sort of place: a country or city (*Spain*, *Cleveland*) or a room (*bathroom*, *kitchen*).

An **EXCLAMATION** or **SILLY WORD** is any sort of funny sound, gasp, grunt, or outcry, like *Wow!*, *Ouch!*, *Whomp!*, *Ick!*, and *Gadzooks!*

When we ask for specific words, like a **NUMBER**, a **COLOR**, an **ANIMAL**, or a **PART OF THE BODY**, we mean a word that is one of those things, like *seven*, *blue*, *horse*, or *head*.

When we ask for a **PLURAL**, it means more than one. For example, *cat* pluralized is *cats*.

MAD LIBS® is fun to play with friends, but you can also play it by yourself! To begin with, DO NOT look at the story on the page below. Fill in the blanks on this page with the words called for. Then, using the words you have selected, fill in the blank spaces in the story. Now you've created your own hilarious MAD LIBS® game!

TYPE OF LIQUID _____

NOUN _____

NOUN _____

VERB (PAST TENSE) _____

PLURAL NOUN _____

PLURAL NOUN _____

PART OF THE BODY (PLURAL) _____

VERB _____

ANIMAL (PLURAL) _____

NOUN _____

VERB (PAST TENSE) _____

PLURAL NOUN _____

PLURAL NOUN _____

ADJECTIVE _____

ADJECTIVE _____

ADJECTIVE _____

NOUN _____

# Adult MAD LIBS®

## A SHORT HISTORY OF ALCOHOL

The world's greatest *drinking* game

---

Just about every culture has made _____ part of life. It's
<br>TYPE OF LIQUID

been around since the _____ Age, the ancient Egyptians
<br>NOUN

took it with them into the after-_____, the ancient
<br>NOUN

Greeks _____ it, and the Babylonians had lots of wine
<br>VERB (PAST TENSE)

gods and _____. No one knows what prehistoric men
<br>PLURAL NOUN

and _____ used to make their drink of choice, but it
<br>PLURAL NOUN

probably gave them the _____ to go out and _____
<br>PART OF THE BODY (PLURAL)     VERB

huge woolly _____. Since then, _____-kind has
<br>ANIMAL (PLURAL)     NOUN

_____ just about everything from honey to _____
<br>VERB (PAST TENSE)     PLURAL NOUN

to corn to make alcohol. While our _____ may have become
<br>PLURAL NOUN

a bit more _____, we're just like our _____ ancestors
<br>ADJECTIVE     ADJECTIVE

in one _____ way—we all love a stiff _____!
<br>ADJECTIVE     NOUN

# RED WINE

The world's greatest *drinking* game

MAD LIBS® is fun to play with friends, but you can also play it by yourself! To begin with, DO NOT look at the story on the page below. Fill in the blanks on this page with the words called for. Then, using the words you have selected, fill in the blank spaces in the story. Now you've created your own hilarious MAD LIBS® game!

ADJECTIVE _____

ADJECTIVE _____

PART OF THE BODY_____

VERB ENDING IN "ING"_____

ADJECTIVE _____

PLURAL NOUN _____

ADJECTIVE _____

TYPE OF LIQUID _____

EXCLAMATION _____

PERSON IN ROOM (FEMALE) _____

PLURAL NOUN _____

NOUN _____

SILLY WORD _____

ADVERB _____

Dear White Wine,

This is your _____ cousin here. I know you think you
              ADJECTIVE

are more _____ and refined, but let's _____
         ADJECTIVE                        PART OF THE BODY

it—you are pale, must be chilled before _____, and
                      VERB ENDING IN "ING"

just don't taste as _____. Plus, the _____ you're
          ADJECTIVE              PLURAL NOUN

served in don't look as _____ as mine. And to be honest,
                  ADJECTIVE

you kind of look like _____. _____! That's gross.
           TYPE OF LIQUID      EXCLAMATION

Also, if a group of women, like _____ and her gang of
                  PERSON IN ROOM (FEMALE)

_____, get together over a/an _____ or two of white
 PLURAL NOUN                    NOUN

wine, all _____ can break loose.
      SILLY WORD

_____ yours,
 ADVERB

Red Wine

# Adult MAD LIBS — WHITE WINE

The world's greatest *drinking* game

MAD LIBS® is fun to play with friends, but you can also play it by yourself! To begin with, DO NOT look at the story on the page below. Fill in the blanks on this page with the words called for. Then, using the words you have selected, fill in the blank spaces in the story. Now you've created your own hilarious MAD LIBS® game!

PLURAL NOUN _____

ADJECTIVE _____

ADJECTIVE _____

ADVERB _____

ADJECTIVE _____

PLURAL NOUN _____

ADJECTIVE _____

ADJECTIVE _____

ADJECTIVE _____

ADVERB _____

PART OF THE BODY (PLURAL) _____

SILLY WORD _____

ADJECTIVE _____

VERB _____

ADJECTIVE _____

PLURAL NOUN _____

Dear Red Wine,

Thank you for your _____, which I presume are due to
_____PLURAL NOUN

the fact that you're feeling _____. You've got it all
_____ADJECTIVE

_____. I am _____ the more _____ of the
ADJECTIVE                          ADVERB                                   ADJECTIVE

two of us. Why, you ask? Well . . . you've been appearing in cheap

_____ with screw caps, and I've even seen you in boxes.
PLURAL NOUN

How _____ for you! Not to mention the fact that you are
_____ADJECTIVE

people's _____ nightmare at a party. If spilled, you create
_____ADJECTIVE

a/an _____ stain that's _____ impossible to get
_____ADJECTIVE                               ADVERB

out. And I won't even mention what you do to people's lips and

_____ when consumed. _____! So you see,
PART OF THE BODY (PLURAL)                        SILLY WORD

_____ cousin, you just can't _____. I'm the
ADJECTIVE                                                          VERB

_____one.
ADJECTIVE

Best _____,
_____PLURAL NOUN

White Wine

MAD LIBS® is fun to play with friends, but you can also play it by yourself! To begin with, DO NOT look at the story on the page below. Fill in the blanks on this page with the words called for. Then, using the words you have selected, fill in the blank spaces in the story. Now you've created your own hilarious MAD LIBS® game!

PLURAL NOUN _____

NUMBER _____

NOUN _____

ADJECTIVE _____

PERSON IN ROOM (MALE) _____

NOUN _____

PERSON IN ROOM (FEMALE) _____

NOUN _____

NOUN _____

CITY _____

NOUN _____

ADJECTIVE _____

PERSON IN ROOM (FEMALE) _____

VERB _____

VERB ENDING IN "ING" _____

ADJECTIVE _____

NOUN _____

# Adult MAD LIBS® PARTY ANIMALS

The world's greatest *drinking* game

---

How many _____ can you put away in a night? More

  PLURAL NOUN

than _____? You might drink more than some of your

  NUMBER

friends, but you probably can't hold a/an _____ to some

  NOUN

of the members of the _____ celebrities club. There's

  ADJECTIVE

_____ Sheen—although he's a complete _____,

PERSON IN ROOM (MALE)                                    NOUN

he claims he's always winning! And we have to mention

_____ Lohan—she must have her own private

PERSON IN ROOM (FEMALE)

_____ in the Los Angeles County _____.

  NOUN                                                    NOUN

_____ Hilton likes to get behind the wheel of a/an

  CITY

_____ once she's been drinking. Not a/an _____

  NOUN                                                    ADJECTIVE

idea. And we have to mention good ole _____

                                       PERSON IN ROOM (FEMALE)

Spears—she tends to _____ a little too much when

                        VERB

she's out _____ a good time. The lesson is—

           VERB ENDING IN "ING"

if you're going to get _____, do it in the privacy of your own

                         ADJECTIVE

_____.

  NOUN

## HANGOVER

The world's greatest *drinking* game

MAD LIBS® is fun to play with friends, but you can also play it by yourself! To begin with, DO NOT look at the story on the page below. Fill in the blanks on this page with the words called for. Then, using the words you have selected, fill in the blank spaces in the story. Now you've created your own hilarious MAD LIBS® game!

VERB _____

PART OF THE BODY_____

ANIMAL _____

NUMBER _____

ADJECTIVE _____

NOUN _____

PLURAL NOUN _____

NUMBER _____

PERSON IN ROOM _____

VERB _____

ADJECTIVE _____

PLURAL NOUN _____

PLURAL NOUN _____

NOUN _____

PART OF THE BODY_____

VERB _____

VERB _____

NUMBER _____

# Adult MAD LIBS HANGOVER

The world's greatest *drinking* game

"I'll never _____ again." Famous last words when you wake
                VERB

up in the morning with your head spinning and your _____
                                                    PART OF THE BODY

feeling like a/an _____ slept on it. The night usually
                      ANIMAL

starts with you saying you'll just go for one. But one turns into

_____. You're having such a/an _____ time! Then it's
   NUMBER                                    ADJECTIVE

your turn to buy the next _____. _____for everyone!
                               NOUN          PLURAL NOUN

Pretty soon it's _____ hours later and you realize you need
                      NUMBER

to go home. You hitch a ride with your friend _____,
                                               PERSON IN ROOM

and somehow manage to _____ into bed. The next morning
                           VERB

is _____. You've got _____ in your hair, you've slept
    ADJECTIVE                  PLURAL NOUN

in your _____, and there's an empty _____ box
          PLURAL NOUN                           NOUN

on your pillow. You drag your _____ to work and do your
                               PART OF THE BODY

best to not _____. You make it through the day—barely.
                VERB

Time to go home and _____ it off. But then you get a text
                         VERB

from your friend—"Hey, let's meet for a drink." Well, maybe just

_____ . . .
   NUMBER

# Adult MAD LIBS TOASTS

The world's greatest *drinking* game

MAD LIBS® is fun to play with friends, but you can also play it by yourself! To begin with, DO NOT look at the story on the page below. Fill in the blanks on this page with the words called for. Then, using the words you have selected, fill in the blank spaces in the story. Now you've created your own hilarious MAD LIBS® game!

NOUN _____

ADJECTIVE _____

NOUN _____

NOUN _____

NUMBER _____

PLURAL NOUN _____

ADJECTIVE _____

VERB _____

ADJECTIVE _____

PERSON IN ROOM _____

NOUN _____

VERB _____

NOUN _____

PLURAL NOUN _____

ADJECTIVE _____

SILLY WORD _____

ADVERB _____

NOUN _____

# Adult MAD LIBS® TOASTS

The world's greatest *drinking* game

---

Everybody likes to raise a/an _____ and toast to the
                                    NOUN

_____ couple, birthday _____, or _____
  ADJECTIVE                         NOUN                NOUN

and wife celebrating their anniversary of _____ years. But
                                              NUMBER

if you are asked to give a toast, there are _____ and etiquette
                                             PLURAL NOUN

you need to follow. Try to keep it _____—you don't want
                                       ADJECTIVE

everyone to _____ off. A/An _____ anecdote can
               VERB                    ADJECTIVE

make a good toast, but know your audience. Stories about how

_____ streaked on the lawn at _____ University
PERSON IN ROOM                            NOUN

might shock Grandma. And don't _____ too much before
                                    VERB

you make your _____. You could end up slurring your
                  NOUN

_____ or saying something _____. If you're nervous,
PLURAL NOUN                          ADJECTIVE

try a simple "_____!" and _____ down your
                SILLY WORD              ADVERB

_____ in one gulp.
  NOUN

MAD LIBS® is fun to play with friends, but you can also play it by yourself! To begin with, DO NOT look at the story on the page below. Fill in the blanks on this page with the words called for. Then, using the words you have selected, fill in the blank spaces in the story. Now you've created your own hilarious MAD LIBS® game!

NOUN _____

NUMBER _____

NOUN _____

ADJECTIVE _____

ADJECTIVE _____

NOUN _____

PLURAL NOUN _____

SILLY WORD _____

ADVERB _____

ANIMAL _____

VERB _____

ADJECTIVE _____

NOUN _____

NOUN _____

NOUN _____

ADJECTIVE _____

PLURAL NOUN _____

NOUN _____

# Adult MAD LIBS®
## ONE FOR THE ROAD
The world's greatest *drinking* game

The bartender has just made the _____ for last call.
NOUN

You should have said good night _____ hours ago.
NUMBER

You're going to have to call your _____-friend and say
NOUN

that you're going to be _____. You better come up with
ADJECTIVE

a/an _____ excuse! But you're still at the _____
ADJECTIVE                                                                NOUN

and you've just bought one more round of _____.
PLURAL NOUN

_____! Will you never learn? You are _____
SILLY WORD                                                               ADVERB

going to be in the _____-house, but you may as well
ANIMAL

_____ that _____ drink. You're certainly used
VERB                        ADJECTIVE

to sleeping on the _____ and not getting any _____
NOUN                                                                  NOUN

for a month. And since you're set on having that one last

_____, it's probably a/an _____ idea to give your
NOUN                                               ADJECTIVE

_____ to the bartender and take a/an _____ home.
PLURAL NOUN                                                        NOUN

From ADULT MAD LIBS®: Ode to Alcohol Mad Libs • Copyright © 2013 by Penguin Random House LLC.

MAD LIBS® is fun to play with friends, but you can also play it by yourself! To begin with, DO NOT look at the story on the page below. Fill in the blanks on this page with the words called for. Then, using the words you have selected, fill in the blank spaces in the story. Now you've created your own hilarious MAD LIBS® game!

PLURAL NOUN _____

ADJECTIVE _____

VERB ENDING IN "ING" _____

PERSON IN ROOM (MALE) _____

ADJECTIVE _____

NOUN _____

ADVERB _____

ARTICLE OF CLOTHING _____

NOUN _____

NUMBER _____

PLURAL NOUN _____

ADJECTIVE _____

ADJECTIVE _____

PERSON IN ROOM (FEMALE) _____

NOUN _____

COLOR _____

# Adult MAD LIBS
## FAMOUS DRINKS
The world's greatest *drinking* game

Movies and TV shows have made certain _____ more
_____ PLURAL NOUN
_____ than the actors and actresses _____ in them.
ADJECTIVE                                    VERB ENDING IN "ING"

One of the most famous drinks is certainly _____
                                            PERSON IN THE ROOM (MALE)

Bond's _____-not-stirred martini. And what about
       ADJECTIVE

the Dude from *The Big Lebowski*'s white _____?
                                          NOUN

It's _____ mandatory to wear a/an _____ while
     ADVERB                                ARTICLE OF CLOTHING

you're sipping that. Who can forget Tony Manero in *Saturday*

_____ *Fever* drinking _____ and Sevens as he discoed
NOUN                            NUMBER

the night away? Or Bridget Jones and her many _____
                                               PLURAL NOUN

of chardonnay? The über-_____ cast of *Mad Men* made
                         ADJECTIVE

_____-fashioneds sexy again. And of course _____
ADJECTIVE                                           PERSON IN THE ROOM (FEMALE)

Bradshaw and her _____-friends from *Sex and the City*
                 NOUN

got everyone drinking a/an _____ cocktail again—the
                           COLOR

cosmopolitan.

# Adult
# MAD LIBS BUBBLES
The world's greatest _drinking_ game

MAD LIBS® is fun to play with friends, but you can also play it by yourself! To begin with, DO NOT look at the story on the page below. Fill in the blanks on this page with the words called for. Then, using the words you have selected, fill in the blank spaces in the story. Now you've created your own hilarious MAD LIBS® game!

NOUN _____

ADJECTIVE _____

ADJECTIVE _____

PLURAL NOUN _____

EXCLAMATION _____

ADJECTIVE _____

SILLY WORD _____

ADJECTIVE _____

TYPE OF LIQUID _____

NOUN _____

ADJECTIVE _____

PLURAL NOUN _____

VERB (PAST TENSE) _____

EXCLAMATION _____

VERB ENDING IN "ING" _____

ADJECTIVE _____

VERB _____

PART OF THE BODY _____

# Adult MAD LIBS BUBBLES

The world's greatest *drinking* game

---

Nothing says "let's celebrate!" more than a/an _____
<br>NOUN

of bubbly! And this _____ drink has a pretty _____
<br>ADJECTIVE      ADJECTIVE

history behind it, too. Supposedly, religious _____
<br>PLURAL NOUN

discovered champagne. _____! Life in that monastery must
<br>EXCLAMATION

have been really _____. But thanks to monks like Dom
<br>ADJECTIVE

_____, the world has this _____ beverage. This
<br>SILLY WORD      ADJECTIVE

delicious _____ can only be called champagne if it comes
<br>TYPE OF LIQUID

from a certain _____ in France. Otherwise it's just plain ole
<br>NOUN

_____ wine. Today more than 200 million _____
<br>ADJECTIVE      PLURAL NOUN

of champagne are _____ every year. _____!
<br>VERB (PAST TENSE)      EXCLAMATION

Better get _____. Just be careful with the cork—they
<br>VERB ENDING IN "ING"

can be _____! You don't want to _____ your
<br>ADJECTIVE      VERB

_____ off!
<br>PART OF THE BODY

From ADULT MAD LIBS®: Ode to Alcohol Mad Libs • Copyright © 2013 by Penguin Random House LLC.

The world's greatest *drinking* game

MAD LIBS® is fun to play with friends, but you can also play it by yourself! To begin with, DO NOT look at the story on the page below. Fill in the blanks on this page with the words called for. Then, using the words you have selected, fill in the blank spaces in the story. Now you've created your own hilarious MAD LIBS® game!

ADJECTIVE _____

PART OF THE BODY _____

TYPE OF LIQUID _____

VERB _____

PART OF THE BODY _____

PLURAL NOUN _____

TYPE OF FOOD _____

PART OF THE BODY _____

ADJECTIVE _____

PLURAL NOUN _____

VERB ENDING IN "ING" _____

PLURAL NOUN _____

ADJECTIVE _____

NOUN _____

PLURAL NOUN _____

VERB ENDING IN "ING" _____

ADJECTIVE _____

ADJECTIVE _____

# HANGOVER CURE

The world's greatest *drinking* game

People will try anything to cure a hangover. Here are some

_____ cures from around the world. Pick your favorite and
   ADJECTIVE

give it a try the next time your _____ is pounding from too
                      PART OF THE BODY

much _____.
   TYPE OF LIQUID

- In Ireland, one cure is to _____ the ailing person up to
                          VERB

  their _____ in wet river _____.
      PART OF THE BODY           PLURAL NOUN

- Puerto Ricans suggest rubbing a slice of _____ on your
                            TYPE OF FOOD

  _____.
    PART OF THE BODY

- A Turkish favorite is _____ soup made from the
                   ADJECTIVE

  stomach of a cow, cooked with _____ and cream. Yum!
                    PLURAL NOUN

- The Russians are convinced that _____ raw _____
               VERB ENDING IN "ING"      PLURAL NOUN

  will make any hangover disappear.

- In Germany, rollmops are thought to be the _____ cure—
                   ADJECTIVE

  but only if you like pickled _____ stuffed with _____.
             NOUN           PLURAL NOUN

Use caution when _____ these _____ cures—they
       VERB ENDING IN "ING"      ADJECTIVE

might just make you more _____!
         ADJECTIVE

# Adult MAD LIBS BEER

The world's greatest *drinking* game

MAD LIBS® is fun to play with friends, but you can also play it by yourself! To begin with, DO NOT look at the story on the page below. Fill in the blanks on this page with the words called for. Then, using the words you have selected, fill in the blank spaces in the story. Now you've created your own hilarious MAD LIBS® game!

ADVERB _____

NOUN _____

NOUN _____

VERB _____

NOUN _____

NOUN _____

ADJECTIVE _____

TYPE OF LIQUID _____

ADJECTIVE _____

VERB ENDING IN "ING" _____

VERB ENDING IN "ING" _____

NOUN _____

ADJECTIVE _____

NOUN _____

PART OF THE BODY _____

ADVERB _____

VERB _____

NOUN _____

# MAD LIBS

### Adult

### BEER

The world's greatest *drinking* game

Beer is the most _____ consumed alcoholic _____
                    ADVERB                                    NOUN

in the world. And no matter where you go in the _____,
                                                         NOUN

you can always get a beer. But what does the beer you _____
                                                              VERB

say about you?

- Blue Moon—Congratulations! You're a total _____.
                                                   NOUN

- Budweiser—You're a/an _____ of _____ taste.
                              NOUN            ADJECTIVE

- Coors Light—Do you like beer at all? Or would you rather have

  a glass of _____?
             TYPE OF LIQUID

- Busch—Be _____. You might be _____ into
              ADJECTIVE                  VERB ENDING IN "ING"

  your dad.

- Labatt Blue—You could be seen as a traitor if you're _____
                                                    VERB ENDING IN "ING"

  beer from north of the _____.
                              NOUN

- Dogfish Head—You could be seen as a/an _____ beer snob.
                                              ADJECTIVE

- Guinness—You are an uncommon _____ with a refined
                                      NOUN

  _____.
  PART OF THE BODY

Choose _____ the next time you _____ a beer. After
           ADVERB                          VERB

all, your _____ is at stake!
              NOUN

# Adult MAD LIBS® PROHIBITION

The world's greatest *drinking* game

MAD LIBS® is fun to play with friends, but you can also play it by yourself! To begin with, DO NOT look at the story on the page below. Fill in the blanks on this page with the words called for. Then, using the words you have selected, fill in the blank spaces in the story. Now you've created your own hilarious MAD LIBS® game!

NUMBER _____

NOUN _____

TYPE OF LIQUID _____

NOUN _____

PLURAL NOUN _____

NOUN _____

ADJECTIVE _____

PERSON IN ROOM (MALE) _____

ADJECTIVE _____

A PLACE _____

ADJECTIVE _____

TYPE OF LIQUID _____

NOUN _____

ADJECTIVE _____

NOUN _____

VERB ENDING IN "ING" _____

PERSON IN ROOM (MALE) _____

NOUN _____

# Adult MAD LIBS  PROHIBITION

The world's greatest *drinking* game

---

Hard to believe that for almost _____ years, you
<br>NUMBER

couldn't get a/an _____ in this country. Worried that
<br>NOUN

_____ was threatening the moral _____
<br>TYPE OF LIQUID    NOUN

and health of the country's _____, Congress passed
<br>PLURAL NOUN

the Eighteenth _____ in 1919, outlawing the sale
<br>NOUN

of alcohol. But that didn't stop _____ gangsters,
<br>ADJECTIVE

like _____ Capone. They smuggled _____
<br>PERSON IN ROOM (MALE)    ADJECTIVE

alcohol from (the) _____ or the Caribbean and served it
<br>A PLACE

in _____ speakeasies. While Prohibition was successful
<br>ADJECTIVE

in reducing the amount of _____ consumed, it led to a huge
<br>TYPE OF LIQUID

_____ in underground and _____ criminal activity.
<br>NOUN    ADJECTIVE

Finally in 1933, the United States _____ passed the Twenty-
<br>NOUN

First Amendment, which ended Prohibition. Upon _____
<br>VERB ENDING IN "ING"

the amendment, President _____ Roosevelt made his famous
<br>PERSON IN ROOM (MALE)

remark, "I think this would be a good time for a/an _____."
<br>NOUN

Now that calls for a drink!

# Adult MAD LIBS  HARD LIQUOR

The world's greatest *drinking* game

MAD LIBS® is fun to play with friends, but you can also play it by yourself! To begin with, DO NOT look at the story on the page below. Fill in the blanks on this page with the words called for. Then, using the words you have selected, fill in the blank spaces in the story. Now you've created your own hilarious MAD LIBS® game!

TYPE OF LIQUID _____

NOUN _____

PLURAL NOUN _____

PERSON IN ROOM _____

PLURAL NOUN _____

ADJECTIVE _____

PLURAL NOUN _____

ADVERB _____

ADJECTIVE _____

NOUN _____

ADJECTIVE _____

VERB _____

NUMBER _____

NOUN _____

ADJECTIVE _____

VERB ENDING IN "ING" _____

TYPE OF LIQUID _____

NUMBER _____

# Adult MAD LIBS® HARD LIQUOR

The world's greatest *drinking* game

So you're not a beer or _____ kind of _____.
                        TYPE OF LIQUID              NOUN

You like to drink the stuff that's in the _____ behind
                                          PLURAL NOUN

the bar. Your friends are named Johnnie Walker, Jim Beam,

Remy Martin, and _____ Cuervo. However, spending
                   PERSON IN ROOM

time with these _____ can sometimes cause things to get
                 PLURAL NOUN

a little _____. Things always start out fine. But after a few
         ADJECTIVE

rounds of _____ you begin to talk _____, tell
           PLURAL NOUN                       ADVERB

_____ jokes, act rude to your best _____, or just
ADJECTIVE                                     NOUN

become _____. Plus, they somehow get you to _____
        ADJECTIVE                                      VERB

at the bar until after _____ a.m., even though you
                        NUMBER

should have been tucked in your _____ hours ago. But
                                 NOUN

without them you wouldn't have met that _____ redhead
                                         ADJECTIVE

_____ at the end of the bar. Thanks, _____—I owe
VERB ENDING IN "ING"                            TYPE OF LIQUID

you _____!
     NUMBER

From ADULT MAD LIBS®: Ode to Alcohol Mad Libs • Copyright © 2013 by Penguin Random House LLC.

# Adult MAD LIBS® YOU CAN DRINK!

The world's greatest *drinking* game

MAD LIBS® is fun to play with friends, but you can also play it by yourself! To begin with, DO NOT look at the story on the page below. Fill in the blanks on this page with the words called for. Then, using the words you have selected, fill in the blank spaces in the story. Now you've created your own hilarious MAD LIBS® game!

EXCLAMATION _____

VERB _____

ADJECTIVE _____

ADJECTIVE _____

NOUN _____

TYPE OF LIQUID _____

ADJECTIVE _____

ADJECTIVE _____

NOUN _____

PERSON IN ROOM _____

NOUN _____

ADJECTIVE _____

NUMBER _____

TYPE OF LIQUID _____

NUMBER _____

VERB _____

ADJECTIVE _____

NOUN _____

# Adult MAD LIBS  YOU CAN DRINK!

The world's greatest *drinking* game

_____! You're finally twenty-one years old and you
<small>EXCLAMATION</small>

can legally _____. How should you celebrate this
<small>VERB</small>

_____ occasion? If you were _____ rich, you
<small>ADJECTIVE</small> <small>ADJECTIVE</small>

and your friends could head to Florida for spring break, have

a wild _____ in Vegas, or go to Germany to drink huge
<small>NOUN</small>

steins of _____ at Oktoberfest. But don't worry—
<small>TYPE OF LIQUID</small>

there are plenty of ways to drink yourself _____ at
<small>ADJECTIVE</small>

home. Try heading to the local _____ bar or throwing
<small>ADJECTIVE</small>

a massive _____ at your best friend _____'s
<small>NOUN</small> <small>PERSON IN ROOM</small>

house. If you decide to throw a/an _____ party, you
<small>NOUN</small>

may need to work on your gymnastics so that you're ready to

do a/an _____ keg stand. And since you're planning on
<small>ADJECTIVE</small>

drinking _____ cups of _____, prepare yourself
<small>NUMBER</small> <small>TYPE OF LIQUID</small>

to run the _____-yard dash to the bathroom. However you
<small>NUMBER</small>

decide to celebrate, try to _____ in moderation. After all,
<small>VERB</small>

you don't want to get so _____ that you don't want another
<small>ADJECTIVE</small>

_____ until you're twenty-two!
<small>NOUN</small>

From ADULT MAD LIBS®: Ode to Alcohol Mad Libs • Copyright © 2013 by Penguin Random House LLC.

# Adult MAD LIBS®  A YEAR OF DRINKING

The world's greatest *drinking* game

MAD LIBS® is fun to play with friends, but you can also play it by yourself! To begin with, DO NOT look at the story on the page below. Fill in the blanks on this page with the words called for. Then, using the words you have selected, fill in the blank spaces in the story. Now you've created your own hilarious MAD LIBS® game!

ADJECTIVE _____

ANIMAL _____

TYPE OF LIQUID _____

ADJECTIVE _____

NOUN _____

PLURAL NOUN _____

ADJECTIVE _____

COLOR _____

TYPE OF LIQUID _____

PLURAL NOUN _____

TYPE OF LIQUID _____

ADJECTIVE _____

VERB ENDING IN "ING" _____

ARTICLE OF CLOTHING _____

VERB _____

ADJECTIVE _____

NOUN _____

# Adult MAD LIBS®  A YEAR OF DRINKING

The world's greatest *drinking* game

Here's a list of _____ holidays to keep you drinking all year long:
<br>ADJECTIVE

**New Year's Day**: You partied hard last night, so try some hair of the

_____ that bit you!
<br>ANIMAL

**Valentine's Day**: Nothing says "I love you" like _____ and chocolates.
<br>TYPE OF LIQUID

**St. Patrick's Day**: Everyone's _____ on the seventeenth.
<br>ADJECTIVE

**April Fool's Day**: You'd be a/an _____ not to drink on the first.
<br>NOUN

**Memorial Day**: It's summer. Break out the white _____ and pants!
<br>PLURAL NOUN

**Father's Day**: Raise a glass to _____ ole Dad, and you might as
<br>ADJECTIVE

well make it his favorite: Johnnie Walker _____ on the rocks!
<br>COLOR

**Fourth of July**: Barbecues, beaches, bikinis, and lots of _____.
<br>TYPE OF LIQUID

**Labor Day**: It's the end of summer. Pack up the white _____
<br>PLURAL NOUN

and pants!

**Halloween**: After a few glasses of _____, you'll realize you're
<br>TYPE OF LIQUID

never too _____ to go trick-or-_____.
<br>ADJECTIVE      VERB ENDING IN "ING"

**Thanksgiving**: Break out your fat _____—it's time to eat
<br>ARTICLE OF CLOTHING

and _____ like you're a/an _____ turkey!
<br>VERB      ADJECTIVE

**Christmas**: It's the _____ that keeps on giving!
<br>NOUN

From ADULT MAD LIBS®: Ode to Alcohol Mad Libs • Copyright © 2013 by Penguin Random House LLC.

# Adult MAD LIBS

## GETTING CARDED

The world's greatest *drinking* game

MAD LIBS® is fun to play with friends, but you can also play it by yourself! To begin with, DO NOT look at the story on the page below. Fill in the blanks on this page with the words called for. Then, using the words you have selected, fill in the blank spaces in the story. Now you've created your own hilarious MAD LIBS® game!

NOUN _____

ADJECTIVE _____

TYPE OF LIQUID _____

PERSON IN ROOM (FEMALE) _____

PART OF THE BODY_____

ADJECTIVE _____

COLOR _____

VERB _____

ADJECTIVE _____

NUMBER _____

TYPE OF LIQUID _____

PLURAL NOUN _____

NOUN _____

PLURAL NOUN _____

VERB ENDING IN "ING"_____

ADJECTIVE _____

ADJECTIVE _____

NUMBER _____

# Adult MAD LIBS® — GETTING CARDED

The world's greatest *drinking* game

Did you ever borrow your older brother's driver's _____
NOUN

or buy a/an _____ ID so you could score that case
ADJECTIVE

of _____ for a party? Or maybe you did what _____
TYPE OF LIQUID                                                    PERSON IN ROOM (FEMALE)

used to do—apply lots of _____ makeup, tease your
PART OF THE BODY

_____ _____ hair, _____ a short skirt and
ADJECTIVE        COLOR                    VERB

_____ heels, and head down to the 7-_____ to try
ADJECTIVE                                              NUMBER

to flirt your way to that bottle of _____. It's also possible
TYPE OF LIQUID

that when you were growing up, there were some _____
PLURAL NOUN

in your town where you didn't have to show any form of

_____ to get in. You just had to make sure your dad's golfing
NOUN

_____ didn't happen to be _____ there! But those
PLURAL NOUN                          VERB ENDING IN "ING"

were the _____ old days—you look your age now, so you're
ADJECTIVE

_____ when someone asks you to prove you're more than
ADJECTIVE

_____ years old!
NUMBER

MAD LIBS® is fun to play with friends, but you can also play it by yourself! To begin with, DO NOT look at the story on the page below. Fill in the blanks on this page with the words called for. Then, using the words you have selected, fill in the blank spaces in the story. Now you've created your own hilarious MAD LIBS® game!

TYPE OF LIQUID _____

TYPE OF LIQUID _____

ANIMAL (PLURAL) _____

NOUN _____

ADJECTIVE _____

NOUN _____

PLURAL NOUN _____

ADJECTIVE _____

TYPE OF LIQUID _____

NOUN _____

NOUN _____

ADJECTIVE _____

ADJECTIVE _____

NOUN _____

TYPE OF LIQUID _____

VERB _____

NUMBER _____

ADJECTIVE _____

Are you sick of drinking beer and wine that tastes like _____?
TYPE OF LIQUID

You could change it up and try fermented _____ from
TYPE OF LIQUID

a mare, or wine made by putting baby _____ in a bottle of
ANIMAL (PLURAL)

rice wine and letting them ferment. Not really the _____
NOUN

you're looking for? Then try *chicha*, one of the most _____
ADJECTIVE

beverages on earth. It's made from kernels of _____ that
NOUN

have been chewed by _____. Sounds _____, right?
PLURAL NOUN                          ADJECTIVE

Or how about snake _____? The Chinese believe
TYPE OF LIQUID

this beverage helps with impotence and _____ loss. The
NOUN

Inuit might win the _____ for the most _____
NOUN                                  ADJECTIVE

alcoholic beverage. Take one _____ seagull, stick it in a/an
ADJECTIVE

_____, fill it with _____, and let it _____
NOUN                    TYPE OF LIQUID              VERB

in the sun. After _____ days, drink up! Hmm . . . Maybe that
NUMBER

beer you're drinking now doesn't taste that _____ after all!
ADJECTIVE

MAD LIBS® is fun to play with friends, but you can also play it by yourself! To begin with, DO NOT look at the story on the page below. Fill in the blanks on this page with the words called for. Then, using the words you have selected, fill in the blank spaces in the story. Now you've created your own hilarious MAD LIBS® game!

VERB (PAST TENSE) _____

NOUN _____

ADJECTIVE _____

PLURAL NOUN _____

ADJECTIVE _____

TYPE OF LIQUID _____

NOUN _____

PLURAL NOUN _____

VERB ENDING IN "ING" _____

NOUN _____

ADJECTIVE _____

NOUN _____

ADJECTIVE _____

VERB _____

ADJECTIVE _____

VERB (PAST TENSE) _____

VERB ENDING IN "ING" _____

NOUN _____

From Dylan Thomas, who _____ into a/an _____ during
                                     VERB (PAST TENSE)                         NOUN

a poetry reading, to Dean Martin, who advised everyone to "Stay

_____," there have been scores of world-class _____.
     ADJECTIVE                                             PLURAL NOUN

Here are a few of the most _____ drinkers in history:
                                   ADJECTIVE

- Ulysses S. Grant—he was dismissed from the military because

  of his love for _____, but still became _____ of
                      TYPE OF LIQUID                        NOUN

  the United States.

- Ernest Hemingway—one of the best _____ of the
                                        PLURAL NOUN

  twentieth century. He had two talents—_____ and drinking.
                                       VERB ENDING IN "ING"

- Johnny Cash—the "_____ in Black," he was so
                                 NOUN

  _____ that he managed to start a/an _____ fire.
     ADJECTIVE                                      NOUN

- Babe Ruth—he would show up _____ to baseball games,
                                  ADJECTIVE

  but still managed to _____ home runs.
                         VERB

- Elizabeth Taylor and Richard Burton—this _____
                                            ADJECTIVE

  Hollywood couple _____ and fought like no one else.
                        VERB (PAST TENSE)

  And they did most of their _____ in public.
                             VERB ENDING IN "ING"

So what do you say—should we have a/an _____ or two in their memory?
                                        NOUN

# KILLER COCKTAIL RECIPE

The world's greatest *drinking* game

MAD LIBS® is fun to play with friends, but you can also play it by yourself! To begin with, DO NOT look at the story on the page below. Fill in the blanks on this page with the words called for. Then, using the words you have selected, fill in the blank spaces in the story. Now you've created your own hilarious MAD LIBS® game!

ADJECTIVE _____

NOUN _____

VERB _____

PLURAL NOUN _____

NUMBER _____

ADJECTIVE _____

ADJECTIVE _____

TYPE OF LIQUID _____

NUMBER _____

PLURAL NOUN _____

NOUN _____

VERB _____

SAME TYPE OF LIQUID _____

VERB _____

NUMBER _____

NUMBER _____

TYPE OF FOOD _____

ADVERB _____

# KILLER COCKTAIL RECIPE

The world's greatest *drinking* game

Why not make your next party really _____ and create your
                                          ADJECTIVE

own _____-tail? Here's a recipe to help you _____
         NOUN                                              VERB

some of those _____ of alcohol you have sitting in the back
                   PLURAL NOUN

of your liquor cabinet. You'll need:

- _____ fluid ounces of _____ vermouth
      NUMBER                         ADJECTIVE

- Three _____ ounces of _____
            ADJECTIVE                TYPE OF LIQUID

- _____ dashes of bitters
      NUMBER

- Two maraschino _____
                      PLURAL NOUN

Directions: Fill a cocktail _____ with ice. _____
                                  NOUN                      VERB

in the sweet vermouth and _____ and _____
                              SAME TYPE OF LIQUID        VERB

on the bitters. Shake while counting to _____. Pour into
                                              NUMBER

_____ cocktail glasses, garnish each with a/an _____
    NUMBER                                                  TYPE OF FOOD

and serve _____.
             ADVERB

MAD LIBS® is fun to play with friends, but you can also play it by yourself! To begin with, DO NOT look at the story on the page below. Fill in the blanks on this page with the words called for. Then, using the words you have selected, fill in the blank spaces in the story. Now you've created your own hilarious MAD LIBS® game!

ADJECTIVE _____

ADJECTIVE _____

VERB _____

NOUN _____

ARTICLE OF CLOTHING _____

PART OF THE BODY _____

NOUN _____

PERSON IN ROOM (MALE) _____

ADJECTIVE _____

VERB ENDING IN "ING" _____

NOUN _____

ADJECTIVE _____

PART OF THE BODY _____

COLOR _____

PART OF THE BODY _____

VERB _____

# PLACES (NOT) TO PASS OUT

Hopefully you'll be _____ enough to pass out in your
                        ADJECTIVE

own bed after a/an _____ night out. But if not, try not
                    ADJECTIVE

to _____ out in a public _____ with your
      VERB                              NOUN

_____ missing. And if your friends _____-cuff
ARTICLE OF CLOTHING                          PART OF THE BODY

you to a/an _____ or street sign, you'll have to channel
              NOUN

_____ Houdini to escape. The police might not think it's
PERSON IN ROOM (MALE)

as _____ as your friends do, and you may find yourself
      ADJECTIVE

_____ it off in a/an _____ at the local police station.
VERB ENDING IN "ING"           NOUN

Or someone might think it's _____ to snap a photo of you
                              ADJECTIVE

and post it on Twitter or _____-book. Mom and Dad will
                          PART OF THE BODY

be so proud of you! And if you think you might _____
                                                COLOR

out at a party, make sure there are no razors or markers around.

You could end up with no _____-brows or looking like
                          PART OF THE BODY

a/an _____-the-dots puzzle!
      VERB

**Adult**
# MAD LIBS
### WORLD-FAMOUS BARS
The world's greatest *drinking* game

MAD LIBS® is fun to play with friends, but you can also play it by yourself! To begin with, DO NOT look at the story on the page below. Fill in the blanks on this page with the words called for. Then, using the words you have selected, fill in the blank spaces in the story. Now you've created your own hilarious MAD LIBS® game!

NOUN _____

ADJECTIVE _____

NUMBER _____

ADJECTIVE _____

TYPE OF LIQUID _____

VERB ENDING IN "ING" _____

ADJECTIVE _____

NOUN _____

ADJECTIVE _____

PERSON IN ROOM (MALE) _____

VERB _____

ADJECTIVE _____

NOUN _____

NOUN _____

NOUN _____

ADVERB _____

ADJECTIVE _____

# Adult MAD LIBS — WORLD-FAMOUS BARS
The world's greatest *drinking* game

There's no shortage of places to drink around the world. So pack your

_____ and let's get started:
NOUN

- Sky Bar—Bangkok, Thailand: Made _____ in the movie
  ADJECTIVE

  *The Hangover, Part II.* You're _____ stories high and only
  NUMBER

  _____ walls separate you and your _____ from
  ADJECTIVE                                          TYPE OF LIQUID

  _____ to your death.
  VERB ENDING IN "ING"

- In 't Aepjen—Amsterdam, The Netherlands: This bar was the

  _____ place of sailors in the 1500s. They paid their
  ADJECTIVE

  _____ tabs with treasure, including monkeys.
  NOUN

- Harry's Bar—Venice, Italy: A/An _____ bar where
  ADJECTIVE

  _____ Hemingway liked to _____, and the place
  PERSON IN ROOM (MALE)              VERB

  where the Bellini, a/an _____ combination of champagne
  ADJECTIVE

  and white _____ juice, was invented.
  NOUN

- White Horse Tavern—New York City: The favorite watering

  _____ of poets, musicians, and writers. Drinkers are
  NOUN

  watched over by a/an _____ of poet Dylan Thomas, who
  NOUN

  _____ died after a whiskey-soaked visit to this _____ bar.
  ADVERB                                                  ADJECTIVE